Maximize Achievement!

Your Future So Bright...
You Gotta Wear Shades!

ACADEMIC READINESS GUIDE TO COLLEGE
COMPLETION AND GRADUATION

Dr. Paul B. Hudson, D.MGT

© 2016 Dr. Paul B. Hudson, D.MGT

All Rights Reserved.

No part of this publication may be reproduced, stored in a retrieval system, or transmitted, in any form or by any means, electronic, mechanical, photocopying, recording, or otherwise, without the written permission of the author.

First published by Dog Ear Publishing
4011 Vincennes Rd
Indianapolis, IN 46268
www.dogearpublishing.net

ISBN: 978-1-4575-4440-8

This book is printed on acid-free paper.

Printed in the United States of America

Table of Contents

1. Dedication v
2. Acknowledgement vii
3. Preface ix
4. Abstract xi
5. About the Book xii
6. Introduction "A College Experience" 1
7. Academic "Grades" Coded Meaning 14
8. *Maximize Achievement!* 26
9. The College perspective 47
10. Conclusion 52
11. References 54
12. Author Biography 56

Dr. Paul B. Hudson is my name
Maximize Achievement! Is my claim to fame.
I'm not new to this game;
I'm true to this game.
I'm in it to win it,
And I intend to play to win.
And nine times out of ten
I'm going to do it again.
Get Back! Get Back! Get Back!
You got to do this
If you want to have stacks!
So work real hard
To get good grades
To make "Your Future So Bright…"
"You Gotta Wear Shades"!
This is sealed for antiquity,
As you make your history;
That leads to your destiny.
And that's all I Got to Say!
Dr. Paul B. Hudson, BBA, MAM, MA, MBA, D.Mgt.

Dedication

My greatest wish is that great academic success will come to all scholars who utilize the *"Maximize Achievement!"* **an Academic Readiness Guide to College Completion and Graduation** to ignite the "Gleam in your bling", making your future bright! Your superior academic achievement endeavors will honor you with the joy of learning, the delight of excellence, and the glory of superior academic success that is earned with your positive mindset when applied to this self-directed, superior academic grades achievement management strategy.

Be excited about your college graduation and career opportunities!

Never let anyone limit what you can do, or be in life; or achieve academically. Those individuals are only critics on the sidelines of your eventual success. Those individuals are not cheerleaders that will encourage your greatness of superior academic achievement. Remember what Theodore Roosevelt said in his speech "Citizenship in a Republic":

> "It is not the critic who counts; not the man who points out how the strong man stumbles, or where the doers of deeds could have done them better. The credit belongs to the man who

is actually in the arena, whose face is marred by dust and sweat and blood; who strives valiantly; who errs, who comes short again and again, because there is no effort without error and shortcomings; but who does actually strive to do the deeds; who knows great enthusiasms, the great devotions; who spends himself in a worthy cause; who at the best knows in the end the triumph of high achievement, and who knows at the worst, if he fails, at least fails while daring greatly, so that his place shall never be with those cold and timid souls who neither know victory nor defeat".

This passage is directed at all the valiant scholars involved in an academic achievement process that requires courage, skill, and tenacity (as opposed to those sitting on the sidelines watching and criticizing).

"Maximize Achievement!" is the academic gift that will keep on giving. Redundancies of thought are inscribed through-out this book to strengthen your continued, ever-evolving pursuit of superior academic grades achievement that will lead to the excitement of college completion and college graduation. *"Maximize Achievement!"*

Acknowledgements

My most gracious praise is extended to the memory of my father; Mr. Johnnie L. Hudson, and mother Mrs. Nannie L. Hudson, for instilling high academic achievement and the love of God to all they encountered. Also, I acknowledge the contributions of Jainean M. Smith; my daughters Andrea P. Hudson and Felecia N. Hudson; my brothers Samuel, Louis, and Steven, and my sisters Nora, Mary, and Rovelma, their children, Morgan, Wellington, Chelsea, Louis, and Jonathon; and the entire Hudson Family clan.

The following master educators and educational professionals set the underlying principles for the creation of this revolutionary, innovative educational management strategy. James Evans Ph.D., Jeffery Haldeman Ph.D., David Brennan Ph.D., John Orr Ph.D., James Brassfield Ph.D., Ray Hinton M.D., Glen Walton Ph.D. Shirley Stansberry Ph.D., Jack Daniels Ph.D., Charlotte Warren Ph.D., Richard McGregory Ph.D., Clarice Ford Ed.D., Christopher Miller Ph.D., Emanuel Newsome Ph.D., Roger Pulliam Ph.D., Ira Rutherford M.S., Ansel Jefferies, M.A., (A.B.D.), Samuel Hudson, M.B.A., Jainean Smith, M.A., John Roberts Ph.D. and Kenneth Durgans, Ed.D.

Also, positive thoughts go out to those striving citizens in my Southwest Michigan hometown of Benton Harbor, Michigan. They have courageously demonstrated the tenacity of a *Tiger* in the face of enduring adversities. *"Maximize Achievement!"*

Preface

Greetings,

The primary purpose of this *"Maximize Achievement!"* is to promote academic achievement and put "the gleam in your bling". It is designed to provide a logical systematic superior, academic grades achievement management strategy. It is an intuitive and practical "how to" methodology for every scholar. These academic management strategies are functional and innovative management efforts are designed to assist educational scholars in achieving educational success both inside and outside of the classroom. This guide will provide all educational scholars with information and the inspirational support strategies needed to enhance a greater chance of superior academic grades achievement success as students pursue the quest of college graduation.

"Maximize Achievement!" will contribute to your positive, sub-conscious, academic mindset. The importance of high level academic goals will be realized in your academic mission as being important; while creating a high priority of a personal necessity of achievement as your academic experience. This structured superior academic grades achievement experience will enhance the capacity of unlimited success and opportunity no matter what the

political, social and economic circumstances. I have personally found this to be true.

"*Maximize Achievement!*" will secure, support and redevelop practical, innovative management strategies to elevate your outcome of academic and career opportunities.

Please let *"Maximize Achievement!"* serve as my official academic appreciation and support of your forthright academic efforts and academic pursuits to successful college graduation. The skills, character and leadership competency herein will guide you as a beacon. Follow its path; it will assist you in your search for superior academic success and superior academic grades achievement. Academic grades achievement creates unlimited options of opportunities.

As a college professor, I personally encourage and invite you to come and share in these self-directed superior achievement strategies through the *"Maximize Achievement!"* are the principles of the functions of management - planning, organizing, leading and controlling people and resources to achieve educational goals. Education is a lifetime opportunity.

Academic life is an adventure; Live it!

Abstract

This book is a management structured educational and academic strategy designed to enhance the positive and reduce the negative academic achievement outcomes of any academic student. The formal management structured within this book, encompasses the basic fundamental functions of management – planning, organizing, leading, and controlling people and resources to guide academic scholars to achieve educational goals.

These four functions of management when initiated by scholars toward academic achievement will instill in the student's subconscious academic mindset, an internal desire of academic achievement. This positive desire will inspire and direct positive academic behaviors; while supporting positive outcome measures for any scholar seeking the pleasure of academic success toward successful college graduation. Read and re-read this guide many times over; is the best way to utilize these positive strategies to the study and execution of any academic class or discipline; and to ultimately bring about your academic achievement goals.

Follow the road of academic success with "Play to win!" *"Maximize Achievement!"*, "Step high!", "Be strong!" and "Be excited!"

About the Book

1. Each time you read any words within this book, you are preparing your mind to learn. Do this by repeating the following dynamic learning affirmation statement daily.

   <u>I intend to play to win!</u> "I am a good student. Any class I study, I can and will do very well. I intend to learn and perform at a high level of superior academic achievement. This is my opportunity in life. I will seize this moment". (Repeat - Affirmation Statement each day)

2. By re-stating this positive affirmation each day before class it will began to be a sub-conscious thought, opening your mind's retention, understanding, and ability to persist through academic circumstances. *"Maximize achievement!"*

3. This book is designed to assist your academic efforts. You can read one word, one line, one paragraph, one page or one chapter and still receive the supporting mental inspiration and guidance to becoming an excelling world class academic performer. Step high!

4. This book is also; designed for you to continuously improve throughout you entire academic college career while pursuing credentials such as, a certificate, associate degree, bachelor's degree, master's degree, or doctoral degree. During your entire academic days, months, semesters, years, (read and reread this guide & repeat the – affirmation in step one. It won't wear out or spoil. Be strong!

5. Don't give up! You are only one thought away from success or failure. This guide is one of the best investments in your academic resource systems. Be excited!

The re-reading, repeating, re-visiting, and re-learning of the affirmation statements is one of the most important strategies in *"Maximize Achievement!"*

It initiate's a self-directed, subconscious, successful academic mindset and way of behaving; and is the foundation of programming the mind to a sub-conscious need and belief of your superior academic achievement possibilities.

This book reinforces and promotes a positive innovative, educational affirmation to all students in order for them to personally embrace the need and value of entertaining risk in order to go beyond their academic expectations. That positive affirmation of the student's confidence, academic skills development and practical academic end-goal solutions is the substance that promotes academic excellence and college completion. The innovative motivational inspiration will contribute to each student's personal buy-in to his or her own academic success. When a student personally accepts the mantle of courage of academic success, he or she will have achieved the impressions, qualities, and factors necessary for the footing of a solid path and move toward successful college completion and college graduation; *"Maximize achievement!"*.

CHAPTER 1
Introduction "A College Experience"

Daily Affirmation

"I am a good student. Any class I study, I can and will do very well. I intend to learn and perform at a high level of superior academic grades achievement. This is my opportunity in life. I will seize this moment".

Greetings! I am a full-time tenured faculty member at Lincoln Land Community College. I serve the college as the Professor of Business within the Business and Technologies Department. One of my demonstrated professional strengths as the Professor of Business is that I believe and teach on the premise that *"all of my students need to be inspired by relevant, supportive, and positive impressions, qualities and value factors"*, to assist the student in academic grade achievement success. Academic grade achievement success is the crucial component needed to propel the student on a solid path that will move them toward college completion.

As with any college student, today's community college students; come to the college environment in many states of mind about their ability, talent, and willingness of achieving academic success. Often college graduation is only a wishful thought in the minds of the students. The students arrive at college with their previous academic experiences as varied as the stars in the night sky. Many of the students are encumbered by the daunting task of uncertainty about their ability or talent in commanding the necessary college success skills. Many times students attend college "just don't know" much about college success or college academic achievement strategies. That is why I sometimes refer to the college environment as the "land of the unknowing".

It is fine for students to come to college "not knowing". It is not fine for them to leave college that way. "Not knowing" **what to do** to achieve academically, **how to** achieve academically and **who is ultimately responsible** for their academic achievement.

As a community college educator, I assume a significant role in assisting the aspiring student with how to know and excel academically, as well as educating and inspiring the student with the attitude, skills and competencies to complete college graduation requirements. Often community college students have the need to be coached, mentored, and influenced to reduce personal fears that prevent them from growing to college graduation. I encourage and inspire an attitude of a willingness to both eliminate the risk of failure and to assume the mantle of their own personal creative educational results. I embrace the task of reinforcing each student's self-responsibility and commitment to his or her academic achievement competency by an ongoing, innovative educational affirmation process. This process begins on the first day of class and continues through the day of class completion, within the thoughts and view of every student. I have coined the affirmation process as *"Maximize Achievement!"*

This book *"Maximize Achievement!"* - reflects my philosophy of nurturing to encourage and inspire impressions of academic success and achievement. The impressions and qualities of *"Maximize Achievement!"* provide the factors and opportunities for each student's individual academic growth and class participation, student leadership programming, and the application of new knowledge with practical strategies to academic solutions and results. The student leadership programming builds a student's self-confidence to compete academically. Without the fear of academic failure or risk aversion, these affirmation processes start students on a solid path and move them toward high-level academic grade achievement and college completion with an attitude of courage. "The gleam in your bling!"

According to Richard L. Daft's - The Leadership Experience, (20015, p.180); "Courage is the mental and moral strength to engage in, persevere through, and with stand danger, difficulty, or fear". Many times these unfounded fears about academic achievement personal prohibit students from college completion. The ability to "step forward" is at times found in terms such as having "backbone", "guts", and fortitude. Those types of human responses; and unfounded fears, are not proof of a student's cowardice, but rather the opportunity for their courage to be demonstrated. In fact, if there were no unfounded fears, courage would not be needed!

A student should accept responsibility for failures and mistakes; rather than avoiding blame or shifting the blame to others. It means non-conformity; going against the grain, and breaking bad academic habits, or reducing academic achievement boundaries and initiating a positive academic change that leads to college graduation. I was made aware of accepting academic responsibility early in my college experience.

Needless to say, I really knew very little about the college academic process and what needed to be done academically to lead to a successful graduation. Besides, college graduation was such a long time away I thought it would happen ... some kind of way, some day. So, I went about it haphazardly, quickly making friends and finding my way around the campus social environment. I didn't feel truly intimidated or completely overwhelmed within the new college academic environment because of my prior college orientation experience of the

Upward Bound program. Upward Bound was a college orientation program that brought high school sophomore, junior and senior students to a college campus during the summer with the hopes of introducing the high school student to the college environment. I knew I was expected to act and respond as a college student; I just wasn't quite sure how to do it completely- to incorporate all of the college nuances and challenges that would lead to college completion.

I entered college at Western Michigan University: as a naïve freshman, three weeks after my high school graduation. I was the first in my family to go away to college. I was excited and awed at the same time. I had visited the campus during the summers of two previous years before graduating from high school. I was in a college orientation program called Upward Bound. It prepared me somewhat for the college experience, but I discovered that actually being in college was different. I was on my own time schedule with responsibility to do everything, make my own daily decisions learn my way in a new environment. The making new friends and acquaintances was an experience that seemed to require more than a casual thought and purpose.

As a first time full time student, I registered for thirteen credit hours of class. I had (three) four credit hour classes and (one) one credit hour class. I knew I shouldn't register for too many credit hours the first semester: otherwise I would be completely swamped in study time. Besides, I thought I still needed to have a little additional time to party and hang out.

I started the classes and attended each faithfully, believing that I was studying and doing everything the right way to successfully attain good (or at least passing grades). During the fourth week of class, we were given the first exams. Afterward, when receiving the first exam results, I observed that my grades results were not as good as I knew they should be. I was at about a "C" average in my courses. I was immediately alarmed by the low grades and knew I had to do *something*. I then realized I didn't quite know what to do or how to raise the grade results.

I began talking with some of my new friends and asking about their grade results, and I soon discovered that they were performing at a higher level. I immediately wondered how that could be. Those individuals didn't seem more intelligent than me, and I believed I was studying as long and hard as they were. Yet my grades were lower than theirs? At least I had the good sense to begin polling and asking them about how to improve my grades and how to do better.

One of my student friends felt some compassion for my dilemma and shared with me some very good suggestions about the process of "college sense "strategies; Some of these that I continue to utilized to this present day to help my own students achieve high academic success in college. That friend informed me that he had received the basic tips and suggestions of how to achieve better grades from his brother and his brother's friends who were about to graduate. He also stated that his brother and the rest were not the smartest or most intelligent students, but they had a simple system that helped them get better grades. It wasn't rocket science, nor was it a secret; it was what I have come to call "college sense". Not a person's common sense, but rather a basic way of approaching and pursuing college academic class success, "college sense" when common sense is not so common.

DO THESE ACTIVITIES TO MASTER COLLEGE COURSE CONTENT:
1. Read all required materials assigned to topics of the class
2. Attend <u>all</u> scheduled class sessions
3. Complete <u>all</u> homework assignments and tests
4. Ask questions <u>in</u> class
5. Join in class discussions
6. Take handwritten notes in class
7. Visit professors at scheduled office hours (office hours are posted)

I listened very closely and wrote down all the suggestions and advice of my many new friends, all the time remembering they were getting better grades than me. Eureka! Those little "college sense" strategies worked wonders for my academic success and college completion. Those same basic little nuggets of information and academic success strategies have helped me successfully complete a bachelor degree, three individual master's degrees and a doctoral degree.

In reviewing my own historical academic achievement success, I began to realize that the academic process strategies and suggestions could help any college student pursuing the college goals of achievement and graduation. I have readily provided many students the "college sense" strategies for many years now with excellent academic success results. To know what to do and how to do it has been the difference between academic success and failure for my students.

Thusly, I have compiled these educational "college sense" strategies and processes within this book to be presented in a format of the formal academic functions of management. Management is the coordination of the resources and people in your academic life in order to achieve your academic goals of college completion. This self-directed academic guide is entitled *"Maximize Achievement!" (College Sense), Academic Readiness Guide to College Completion and Graduation.*

"*Maximize Achievement!*" is a management strategy that can and will improve your academic achievement success. These academic achievement management concepts, processes and strategies are intended to be the guidelines to instruct and position you to win academically both in and out of formal academic institutions. Think: "positive results".

The goal of the academic achievement management strategy is simply to identify superior academic grades achievement. Those grades are the formal measures of your academic achievement for world-class performance. The reflection of your academic grades achievement will create the brilliance of your future academic and career opportunities, thusly providing, "the gleam in your bling".

This book is designed to be an academic support tool; a practical "how to" methodology for assisting the college student in the task of brightening his or her future opportunities. Such great future academic and career opportunities are realized through world-class performance that provides the student with a realization of excellence in the attainment of superior academic grades achievement. The overriding purpose of the academic achievement management strategies is to inform, persuade, and remind the academic student of the art of securing the highest academic grades levels as possible.

The prescribed academic management functions activities and tasks are proven academic success models that I have employed by successfully for more than thirty years to counteract the result of failure and low academic grades performance outcomes.

Failure should not be an option! According to *Study Tactics: A Master Plan for Success in School,* some people claim that their failure in academic subjects, is a lack of aptitude for the subjects, saying they just cannot learn mathematics or foreign languages (to name two of the most commonly quoted subjects). (Armstrong, W.H., and Lampe II [New York: Barron's Educational Series, 1983].98). While it is true that some people do have such low aptitudes for certain subjects so as to prevent their success, most people can overcome low aptitude by hard work. Most failure in school subjects comes from failure to study enough or to study in the proper way. Thus, your habits of work will be significant factors in determining the grades you earn. All your knowledge about time planning, study methods, note taking, and spelling will be of little use unless you put that knowledge to work. For every subject, you will have to make minor adaptations to your study methods so as to emphasize the areas of the subject in which you need to concentrate most of your efforts and management strategies.

As explained in <u>Management: Leading & Collaborating in a Competitive World,</u> is the process of working with people and resources to accomplish organizational goals. (Batemen, Thomas, and Scott Snell [New York: McGraw Hill/Irwin, 2013, p.14), Bateman & Snell (2013, p.14). Both the instructional and performance technologies are subsets of an even larger domain. Most management strategy involves the allocation and control of available resources toward the accomplishment of goals and objectives. No matter whether we are talking about the management of a giant corporation, a ship, a church, a family, a classroom, or even our own personal academic lives; we are talking about "allocating and controlling available resources to accomplish goals and objectives" (Mager, Robert F.,<u>Making Instruction Work</u>[New Jersey: Center for Effective Performance, 1988], p.9).

The formal management process and strategy is realized through four basic fundamental actions and activities known as "the functions of management". The four principle functions of management are planning, organizing, leading, and controlling and will provide an efficient and effective manner for students to achieve academically. Thusly, when these four functions of management are applied to the academic discipline, they are known as the "academic achievement management strategies". These specific strategies for academic management processes are designed to lead academic scholars to the goal of achieving academic success and superior academic grade achievement. These superior academic grades achievement management strategies consist of self-directed planning, organizing, leading and controlling the resources and innovations in the academic environment that support superior academic success. The student ultimately must be the force that initiates and sustains the actions, energy, and drive toward academic achievement. *"MAXIMIZE ACHIEVENET!"* is the rudder that directs the successful path and accomplishment of desired academic performance. Academic management provides the student with a competitive advantage that lights the way to unlimited prosperity and opportunities through the attainment of formal measures known as superior academic grades. Academic grades management is the actions and activities applied by the student to earn a level of desired academic performance on the grading scale of recognized academic and career opportunities.

The power revealed in this book is structured into five component segments of understanding and comprehension that underlie the attainment of superior academic grades achievements. The component segments of this book are:

1. INTRODUCTION
2. ACADEMIC "GRADES"
3. ACADEMIC "GRADES" CODED MEANINGS
4. THE EDUCATIONAL MANAGEMENT PROCESS
5. THE COLLEGE PERSPECTIVE.

Each of these component segments includes brief descriptions and scenarios that are equally significant in establishing mental structures and practical strategies to build a student's world-class performance. *"Maximize Achievement!"* is a self-directed attitude builder for superior academic grades achievement results in the attainment of successful college graduation, by the student as a committed, deliberate, and enduring scholar. *"Maximize achievement!"*

CHAPTER 2
ACADEMIC GRADES

Daily Affirmation

"I am a good student. Any class I study, I can and will do very well. I intend to learn and perform at a high level of superior academic grades achievement. This is my opportunity in life. I will seize this moment".

Academic grades represent the formal standardized measures of the interpretations of the proficiency and levels of comprehension of a student within a class or subject area. The interpretation of the proficiency level of a student and/or educational participant is usually done by persons responsible for overseeing and presenting the content of a class or session. The authoritative person or individuals is known as an instructor, teacher, professor, or coordinator and has the right and responsibility to quantify, code or set the criteria to reflect the interpreted proficiency or level of comprehension identified of a student's output. These evaluations of the proficiency and level of comprehension are determined by objective and subjective evaluation of the students' performance output data earned within the context of the class requirements. An accumulation of the performance output data such as tests, topic assignments, class participation, research papers, oral and written presentations and value credits (sometimes known as "extra credit") is the results of the collective interpretation criteria of the persons in charge of the class, group or seminar.

Educational academic grading in most colleges and universities in the United States is typically represented by five alphabetical letters: **A, B, C, D,** or **F,** with an **(A)** being the highest level of proficiency and comprehension of the subject area, (academic mastery) known as ("excellent"). An **(F)** is the lowest level of proficiency and comprehension of the subject area, meaning a failure and lack of academic mastery; (sometimes termed "to flunk" the class or subject matter).

The mission and goal of all students is to achieve as high a level of superior academic grades as possible in all subject matter attempted. Hopefully all **(A's)** or as close as possible is the results in every class, lecture, lab, or session. Academic achievement is then the process of how a student is attaining or maintaining a desired high level of performance status within the formalized academic environment. Academic achievement is the continuous progression of the student measurements within and throughout the formal academic environment. This is the desired recording of the performance of class information, knowledge, and intellect that leads to excellent results and outputs. Thus, these measures are the valuable resources and unlimited opportunities that are attained by the student scholar. This precious bounty is the essence of your enlightenment and enrichment value: The gleam in your bling! You make it shine!

CHAPTER 3
ACADEMIC "GRADES:" CODED MEANINGS

Daily Affirmation

"I am a good student. Any class I study, I can and will do very well. I intend to learn and perform at a high level of superior academic grades achievement. This is my opportunity in life. I will seize this moment".

Again, superior academic grades achievement is the standardized measures of the student's present academic achievement and the present reality for his or her future opportunities and future wealth status, making the serious point that academic grades are a valuable resource and, when obtained and utilized properly, will contribute to the student's present and future prosperity and opportunities.

Most of the time, many students may not understand or consider that the life-time inherent value of superior academic grades achievement is as valuable as the money they spend or invest. The meaning of investment is that there should be a positive return on whatever the valuable resource that is initially put at risk or employed in an endeavor. This inherent value-added benefit of high academic achievement gives the valid reasons for the student to strive with as much effort as can be initiated, whereas to establish a positive outcome of a significant valuable return. It is almost an axiom that is spoken by most college faculty, that a student's future earning ability and reality is highly correlated to academic grades achievement. These successful academic grades achievements ultimately lead to certifications, diplomas, and degrees awarded through academic and commercial institutions.

Remember academic grades are "lifelong" judgments or snapshots of who the student is and how the student's capabilities have been recognized by the score-keepers of historical academic performance results. Many times, students and/or educational participants do not fully realize or consider the critical impact of the score-keepers' records. Whether in the present or in the future, when a student applies for a career position, seeks higher educational opportunities, or is evaluated against opposing candidates, the historical record of the score-keepers' (records known as "transcripts") will be requested by the interested parties, schools, colleges and employers. The records or transcripts are an accumulation of all academic grades achievements and scores that are on or in the student's files stored, held, and maintained at the academic institution in the "registrar's office". The "registrar's office" of most colleges and academic institutions is usually the holder and disseminator of all official academic records of a student and/or educational participant. These stored, recorded and disseminated historical transcripts can be requested by any source or interested party as an "official transcripts". Such transcripts are only noted to be "official transcripts" when forwarded from the registrar office directly to the interested parties and, sealed in an official college envelope that is unopened and untouched by the student in any manner.

Students should regularly audit and review all historical records stored in the "registrar's office" during and after the enrollment period at any academic institution attended. A student should know about any information that is being forwarded to anyone about or concerning his or her official academic records.

The student's academic grades achievements about subjects, (discipline) majors, minors, diplomas, certifications, degrees, and graduation status are routine request by interested parties. The academic grades achievements kept on file in the registrar's office will be a letter grade of (A, B, C, D, E, F or I-for incomplete or Cr. for Credit), of all classes attempted and/or completed at the academic institutions. These historical letter designations associated with academic grades achievement performance represent the spectrum of A=excellent superior performance to F=failure or flunk. The registrar's office will maintain these academic grades achievement records forever. So, make sure the academic grades achievements are worthy to represent the best you and reflect the person you are capable of being at present and in the future.

Within the frame work of the student's historical academic achievement performance it would do well for him or her to review and decode the meaning of all academic grades achievements as valuable resources and doors of unlimited opportunity. I have found through questioning students that many times students do not realize the true meanings of the letter grades and what the letter grades represent. The reality of academic grades with many students is much like the imaginative reality of the Easter Bunny, the Tooth Fairy, Santa Claus, or the Wizard of Oz; the reality is only a figment of imagination, nothing that is real, fixed or concrete. We believe that we know who and what these imaginative manifestations are, but they really only exist in our minds. Many times I, as a professor, have asked students, "How are you doing in their classes?" I receive responses such as, "I'm doing O.K." or "I'm doing alright". But I have personally never submitted a grade in college called "Okay" or "alright". Think of letter grades as having true meaning and a fixed, concrete reality as to the following realities of your opportunities in life scenarios:

A's: - All opportunities are available
B's: - Opportunities can be O.K.
C's: - Cut your opportunities
D's: - Don't think about opportunities
F's: - Forget about any opportunities
I's: - Incomplete (no potential opportunity or failure)

A responsible student should realize the extent to which his or her current and future academic and career opportunities may and will be determined by these letter academic grades achievement performance designations. There should be a renewed urgency for the student to know the status of his or her academic grades achievement performance history on formal transcripts. A concerned student will have continued knowledge of his or her academic letter grade success. This knowledge will keep the student on the path of success.

<u>Coping with college: A Guide for Academic Success</u> asserts that "success is a journey", <u>(Hamachek, A. L. [New Jersey: Pearson Education Inc., 2001] p.11)</u>. Sometimes the journey will be easy, and sometimes it will be hard. When you encounter bumps and barriers, inspiration and motivation will help you stay on the path. If you get overwhelmed and the world seems a little dark, read and reflect on these words of wisdom, and enjoys, a triumphant journey. See yourself through the darkness

with the visionary, ambitious, desirable future. Remember the saying from an old English churchyard:

> "Life without vision is drudgery. Vision without action is but an empty dream. Action guided by vision is joy and the hope of the earth". (as quoted in Daft, Richard, The Leadership Experience[Independence, KY: Cengage Learning, 2014],p.304).

Please note that it is your personal responsibility as the student to be interested. No one can be interested for you, and no one can increase your interest unless you will it. That is the basic obligation you must take to class; and the basic obligation you must hold up to each assignment. In life it is the basic obligation that you will carry into your life's work, or life will make you a person of no consequence or influence, going from job to job, thinking that the grass will be greener on the other side of the fence, bored with things as they are because you were never interested enough to learn that it is only through ignorance that we become bored.

Do not expect that all assignments or even all subjects to hold a natural interest for you. Mastering a subject that does not appeal to you will give you confidence in your ability to do difficult things as you go through life. Life is full of little duties that carry no immediate appeal, but the person who can tackle a job whether he or she likes it or not is a successful, happy one.

As stated in *Study is hard work: The most Accessible and Lucid Text Available on acquiring and Keeping Study Skills through a Lifetime:*

> Your effort and will cannot be reduced to a simple formula or practice; interest cannot be learned as one learns vocabulary or a law of science. Interest can be acquired best, perhaps, by starting with a determination that there is scarcely any limit to what a human being can do if he is sufficiently interested. And if one is sufficiently interested, the burdensome drudgery of study and work disappear. Then one experiences appreciation and deep feeling (Armstrong, [Boston: David R. Godine, Publisher, 1967] p.95).

And if one is sufficiently interested, as Armstrong and Lampe point out, the burdensome drudgery of study and work disappear. Then one experiences appreciation and deep feeling.

Pauk and Owens assert that:

Taking control of your classes and assignments means viewing them as choices instead of obligations. The stressed-out, overwhelmed student looks to the next lecture or reading assignment with dread. The student who feels in control (and confident as a result) understands that he or she attends lectures and completes assignments as a matter of choice and that the benefits derived from both are not only practical but also enjoyable.

According to psychologist Mihalyi Csikszentmihalyi, "Of all the virtues we can learn, no trait is more useful, more essential for survival and more likely to improve the quality of life than the ability to transform adversity into an enjoyable challenge". (*Flow: The Psychology of Optimal Experience* [New York: Harper Perennial Modern Classics, 1991] p.200)

Maximize Achievement!

(College Sense)

*PLANNING: – PLAY TO WIN!

*ORGANIZING: – MAXIMIZE ACHIEVEMENT!

*LEADING: – STEP HIGH!

*CONTROLLING: – BE STRONG!

*YOUR ACADEMIC GOALS: – BE EXCITED!

CHAPTER 4

Maximize Achievement!

Daily Affirmation

"I am a good student. Any class I study, I can and will do very well. I intend to learn and perform at a high level of superior academic grades achievement. This is my opportunity in life. I will seize this moment".

Maximize Achievement! – is your coordination of actions, people, and resources in order to achieve your desired goals of superior academic grades achievement success. The actions and activities of a student are the basic functions or "what you do" to achieve desired academic results. Many academics focus on agendas such as "time management" as being the key component to college academic success. Scharf and Hait acknowledge that actually, the term "time management" is paradoxical, (<u>Studying Smart: Time Management for college students New York: Harper & Row, 1985])</u> In fact, time is a fixed quantity. It is always there, always the same. Time cannot be bought or sold. It must be spent; it can't be saved. Time can't be lost or found. The only variable you have is how you choose to spend those 86,400 seconds every day.

Time management really means learning how to manage *yourself* with respect to the finite reality of time.

This overall model of *Maximize Achievement!* expresses the same "time management" reality and focusses on "what you should do" within the formal functions of management of using the four basic applied "functions of management":

Maximize Achievement! is the coordination of all actions, people and resources to achieve academic goals of superior academic grades achievement success.

- **FUNCTIONS:** – Self-directed actions –that students use to achieve academic goals
- **PLANNING:** – Activities and actions that lead to academic grades achievement
- **ORGANIZING:** – Being effective and efficient in your efforts to pursue excellence
- **LEADING:** – Vision and ability to influence yourself to end goals
- **CONTROLLING:** – Set standards of performance and taking corrective actions

These four component functions of the formal management process are - planning, organizing, leading and controlling are the performance criteria that allow students to prepare themselves to achieve the task of superior academic grades achievement enhancement. Each of these four functions of *Maximize Achievement!* directs the student's actions, activities, and decisions, whereby his or her self-directed, initiated strategies will lead to the desired results of superior academic grades achievement success and college completion through graduation.

(Change Model)
Unfreeze>Move>Refreeze

Please consider that change in academic achievement is a self-determined and self-driven result by you, the student. Motivate yourself to change. When you change your behaviors to bring about desire, will and can become your desired academic reality. Change in all phases of your life is inevitable. But rather than simply going through the change, began to *direct the change* to your academic achievement future. Deal with your resistance to positive change.

As stated by (Bateman and Snell 2013) "People must come to recognize that some of the past ways of thinking, feeling, and doing things are obsolete. (*Management*) You must break out of or <u>*unfreeze*</u> your present non-desired mode of thinking, feelings and doing things; <u>*move*</u> your reality by instituting things that lead to your success; <u>and finally</u> <u>*refreeze*</u> your desired behavior by reinforcing and supporting your thinking, <u>feeling</u> and doing <u>by</u> new behaviors of success.

Remember that there is always a natural resistance to change. So you must identify the forces that prevent you from a desired academic achievement change and practice those that lead you to your desired academic achievement goals. Take charge of your academic achievement life and begin to direct your academic achievement change, rather than simply going haphazardly through the academic changes, just wishing for desired results to just happen. Maximize achievement!

Remember, you possibly have always experienced too much of "too little academic success". Now it is time to create something from nothing. Your attitude and effort are limitless resources to motivate you to achieve successful college graduation.

"PLANNING:"

"I

INTEND

TO

PLAY TO

WIN!"

The planning function of *Maximize Achievement!* systematically makes decisions about the activities that an individual, group, work unit, or overall organization will pursue that lead to goals (Bateman and Snell,

Management, 2013 p. 14). The academic grade planning process is to establish goals and decide which activities will lead to enhanced superior academic grades achievement. This academic readiness planning activity is presented in a step-by-step sequential process to further the student's understanding of class and comprehensive knowledge of course content. These are study activities and methods relative to the course content and participation. The planning process is the excellence of preparation. As explained by Armstrong and Lampe II, (1983, p. 50) "expect new study methods to produce new results". You must be convinced that better habits will (a) help you find what you are expected to learn, (b) understand it more rapidly, (c) fix it in your mind more easily, and (d) improve your recitation and grades (*Study Tactics*, 50). Once convinced, discipline yourself aginst the hazards of learning. One that is typical and causes many muddled and incorrect answers is that of trying to cram at the beginning of class, sometimes even while the teacher is making an announcement or assignment. Such an act betrays either lack of preparation or lack of confidence. The impression made by such practice upon the teacher is one of indifference to good habits of a specific study plan and poor planning.

Nist-Olejnik and Holschuh emphasizes that perhaps the biggest advantage of a good specific study plan is actually in creating it. It has been the author's experience that most students benefit more from creating a structured plan than from one that's just in the student's heads (<u>College Success Strategies</u> [New Jersey; Prentice Hall, 2011] p.172). Creating a plan and clipping it in your daily planner reminds you that you have set aside specific times to rehearse and review and enables you to be ready on test day. The specific study plan also allows you to evaluate how your plan is working and to modify it if things are not proceeding as you thought they would. Finally, your specific study plan outlines not only when you will study but also the strategies you will use, requiring you to put more thought into your plan beyond just scheduling the time of your study sessions. For example, it shows when you plan to meet with your study group so that you can prepare in advance.

The lifestyle and academic rigors of college life require great discipline as an independent learner. In college, there is no one to get you to your classes, to see that you are not late, to be sure you have done your assignments, or to help you with such personal activities as doing your laundry, cleaning your room, and paying your bills. Becoming an independent learner takes some time, but it also requires certain skills (Hamacheck, <u>Coping with College</u>, 2002, p.6).

(Zwier and Mathes, 2005) agrees that critical thinking is exercised as students evaluate the usefulness of certain strategies to successfully achieve high-level academic requirements. (Study Skills for Success [Michigan: University of Michigan Press, 2005).The following are some suggestions as to the mastery of course content strategies within any class taken at any college:

DO THESE ACTIVITIES TO MASTER COLLEGE COURSE CONTENT:
1. Read all required materials assigned to topics of the class
2. Attended all scheduled class sessions
3. Complete all homework assignments and tests
4. Ask questions in class
5. Join in class discussions
6. Take handwritten notes in class
7. Visit professors at scheduled office hours (office hours are posted)

DO THESE PLANNED STRATEGIES FOR HIGH GRADE PERFORMANCE:

1. Sit in the front row of your class or "T-Zone"(the near middle of the class)
2. Arrive to class 20 minutes before class starts

3. Make the acquaintance of the professor – (remember office hours)
4. Buy textbooks early and read assignments early
5. Manage a consistent study time – (find the time)
6. Do reports, papers and projects ahead of due date
7. Identify and partner with high achievers –("birds of a feather, flock together")
8. Be true to yourself – know yourself, and be willing to develop
9. Don't be a participant of a "pity party" – ("misery loves company")
10. Achieve a superior (4.0) academic grade point

"I intend to PLAY TO WIN!" - is a positive reinforcement phrase to emphasize the value of planning that will help you <u>master college course content</u> and <u>plan strategies for grade performance</u> to facilitate academic goal achievement in any class of study. Academic <u>planning</u> in its simplest form is to establish your college graduation goals and <u>decide</u> what actions and activities to initiate to accomplish those academic goals. I believe planning is often the "first step" in the management functions because all other management functions depend on an effective planning process. This planning process is imperative to achieve success in all college class efforts: the traditional classroom, the online class, the directive study <u>and the</u> independent study class.

"ORGANIZING":

Maximize Achievement!

The organizing function of *Maximize Achievement!* prioritizes the "assembling and coordinating human, financial, physical, informational, and other resources needed to achieve goals" (Bateman and Snell, <u>Management</u>). As stated by Pride, Hughes, and Kapoor, "Organizing is the grouping of resources and activities to accomplish some end result in an efficient and effective manner" (<u>Business</u>[Boston, MA: Houghton Mifflin Co., 2012, p.173</u>). For the academic student to accomplish an effective and efficient manner in the constant pursuit of superior academic grades achievement is a very daunting and critically-structured effort of personal preference and design.

Remember: Your ultimate job in college is to be a student. You will want to be a good one! The goal of all educational instruction is learning. Learning is commonly defined as a change in behavior. You likely have learned how to tie your shoes, write your name, and drive a car. These were things that at one time you did not know how to do. However, you learned and, thus your behavior changed. You now know how to do those things. For the most part, the challenge isn't learning;

itself. You have great ability to learn, you likely wouldn't have made it to college. More likely, academic problems occur when your learning system isn't efficient and effective (Hamachek, <u>Coping with College,</u>2002, p.7). Below are some resource suggestions to becoming a more efficient and effective student. The mastering of these resources will be one of the most important academic achievement strategies you will ever achieve. Organizing will lead you to the accomplishment of even the most difficult academic achievement goals.

EFFICIENT & EFFECTIVE USE OF RESOURCES- (Time, Self, Activities, & Money):

1. Time Management: – there are twenty-four hours in a day
2. The reading of textbooks
3. Memory techniques
4. Test taking: – breath and relax before taking a test
5. Effective communication
6. Expect high academic achievement
7. Attend learning labs & study tables
8. Sufficient financial planning: – college students are always poor
9. College grade replacement policy: – know what it is and how it works

10. Be organized In your value of priorities (assess strengths and weaknesses)
11. Self-talk (the daily mirror effect)

"Maximize Achievement!" - is the positive reinforcement phrase to emphasize the most <u>efficient and effective use of resource</u>, for the utilization of all your tangible or intangible value. *Organizing* is the grouping of all resources necessary to accomplish the attainment of the high- level academic end results or goals. Remember: All resources are valuable and should be utilized to their highest advantage.

"LEADING:"

STEP HIGH!

The <u>leading function</u> of *Maximize Achievement!* involves the manager's <u>ability</u> to stimulate high-level desired performance by employees (Bateman and Snell, <u>Management</u>, p. 15) This phenomenon is also explained by Pride, Hughes, and Kapoor as "the process of influencing people to work toward a common goal" (Business, 2012, p.173). Many times most understanding of leading is related to followers. Within the context of personal academic achievements, however, the identification of leading is a reality of being able to lead one's own personal values and activity to achieve desired superior academic grades achievement goals.

Koch & Wasson acknowledges that values are standards by which we judge ourselves and others (<u>The Transfer Student's Guide to the college Experience [Boston, MA: Houghton Mifflin Co. 2002, p.149</u>. <u>Values</u> are also standards by which we set priorities; that is, we have learned or developed a hierarchy of values that govern our goal-seeking behavior. A goal is a desired outcome to be attained in the future. Goals are frequently observed in our choice of occupation or profession. As an example, let's say I have a goal of helping people get well. My values or motivation <u>are</u> altruistic and nurturing, and I therefore attach a high priority to obtaining a medical degree so that I may exercise my values. This means that other goals, such as beginning a family or traveling, may have to be postponed: – a process known as "delayed gratification". In this way, our values and motives actually help us determine our goals and the priorities we assign to them. Our behaviors are the vehicles that put our values in action and carry us to our goals.

You may not realize it, but you are always motivated to do something. No matter where you are or what you are doing, *you are always motivated to do something*, even if it's just sleeping. Focusing your motivation on learning, however, may sometimes be challenging. It is important to understand that you are responsible for your own motivation, even in courses you don't like. The current thinking on motivation can be summed up by saying that motivation is not something that is done *to* you; in other words, no one can motivate you but *you*. Others can provide stimuli, explaining, for example, the reason *why* it is important to learn biology even though you plan to major in literature. But in the end, the motivation must come from you. Thus, although an interesting instructor may make it easier for you to stay motivated, no one can directly motivate you to learn. But given that you are always motivated to do something and that you are primarily responsible for your motivation, there are some differences between students who are motivated to learn and students who are not (Nist-Olejnik and Holschuh, College *Success Strategies*, 2011 p.40) Within this book, are suggested personal self-leading values that will enable a person the motivation to lead himself or herself in a direction of a desired positive academic goal achievement.

YOUR PERSONAL VALUES INFLUENCE THE LEADING OF YOURSELF:

College offers a time to reflect on the purpose of learning and to the uses in which you will put your knowledge. Values are a central element of this reflection. In addressing a college graduating class, the creator of the Doonesbury comic strip, Gary Trudeau, described as "permanently professionalized" and "chillingly competitive". He chided students for their "obsessive concern for the future," seen as "the salient shaping influence on your attitudes during a very critical four years". He went on, "IT could have been more than that. This college offered you a sanctuary, a place to experience *process*, to *feel* the present as move through it, to *embrace* both the joys and sorrows of moral and intellectual maturation! It needn't have been just another way station".

The college years provide an essential opportunity to experience values development of what Trudeau called "process". Embracing values that will enhance your life will be one of the most important outcomes of your college experience. The first year of college is the optimal time to begin this process (Gardner, J.N., A.J. Jewler, Betsey Barefoot, *Your College Experience, Strategies for Success* [Belmont, CA: Wadsworth/Thomson Learning 2004, p.125)].

LEAD YOUSELF TO AN ACADEMIC GOAL of COLLEGE GRADUATON!
1. Visualize college graduation: – see your compelling desirable academic future

2. Mission: – your basic academic scope and academic purpose
3. You are unique and different from any other student: – with unique strategies
4. Academic grades: – end goals you project and expect to achieve
5. You are an adult: – Be responsible!
6. Academic grades are very serious precise outcomes measures with consequences, work closely with college academic advisors
7. The "Gleam in your bling":- the reality of your future opportunities
8. Two way self-communication model: – Step high! Be excited!

STEP HIGH! is the positive reinforcement phrase to emphasize the necessary process while consistently, continually, and positively influencing yourself to work toward your academic goal of college graduation. The visualization of a compelling, desirable future will assist you, the scholar, to be motivated with a sustainable drive and effort toward your academic goal of college graduation. Your focused positive conscious and sub-conscious thoughts will direct your actions and activities through the difficulties and restraints during the process of goal attainment.

"Power is the potential ability of one person to influence…influence yourself to bring about desired outcomes" (Daft, Richard, *The Leadership Experience* [Independence, KY: Cengage Learning, 2014, p.369). And work is defined by *The American Heritage Dictionary of The English Language* as "physical or mental effort or activity directed toward the production or accomplishment of something" (1992, p.2056).

Please understand that all production and accomplishment of a great goal requires work. Ultimately you, the student scholar, must be responsible for <u>your</u> academic destiny. You have the potential ability to bring about your high-level academic desired results. Be prepared to do great work, if you desire great opportunities. *Maximize Achievement!* - The gleam in your bling!

"CONTROLLING:"

BE STRONG!

The controlling function of *Maximize Achievement!* is monitoring, evaluating, and regulating performance and making needed changes to ensure desired goal attainment (Bateman and Snell, *Management,* p.16)As further explained by Pride, Hughes, and Kapoor, *Business*, 2012 p.174) "controlling is the process of evaluating and regulating ongoing activities to ensure that goals are achieved". Measure the actual performance and take the necessary corrective actions to ensure your academic goal is attained. The monitoring of your superior academic grades achievement performance is a crucial step in implementation of a true management strategy to improve or achieve the desired academic goals. "Monitoring" means to evaluate one's current academic performance and make decisions as to the position of that performance. Once the monitoring process is concluded, and one understands the actual current academic performance reality, the next process is to set a desirable goal standard and then monitor the progress of that standard. The controlling process is ongoing and will accommodate the attainment of academic success.

ALWAYS EVALUATE YOUR ACADEMIC PERFORMANCE STANDARDS:

1. Always be conscious of your current academic grades performance
2. Realistic academic goals: –stretch (this not readily attainable)
3. Evaluate history, opportunities, and destiny
4. The one who thinks he/she can

5. Continuous evaluation process (always meet with professors & academic advisors)
6. Be true to yourself

PLEASE TAKE CORRECTIVE ACTIONS & DEVELOP THE WILL TO PREPARE!

From *Barron's Pocket Guide to Study Tips:*

Perception and preparation without *thought* brings neither conscious purpose nor action. The gift of thought is the one without which all other gifts lie dormant. Your whole education is designed to bring growth to your ability to think. If this were not so, the number of puzzles that increase with each year of your life would overwhelm you. The gift of thought provides the human mind to deal in abstractions. A sound, for example, is an abstraction that can be converted into deep feeling. It can also be made into a symbol – a spoken word. Man has the ability to record the spoken word by writing and making it visible. The gift of thought makes possible all the valuable things that make our world: material things, ranging from the first flint hatchet of the cave man to the most advance rocket; and immaterial things –

religion and morals, institutions such as home and community, and qualities and standards (Armstrong, William[NewYork: Barron's Education Books, 2004,p.3]).

The goal is for you to instill a positive, self-directed "subconscious thought" that stimulates an automatic, inspired, and positive outcome.

1. Instill positive "subconscious thought" daily
2. Have some shame of failure
3. Have no <u>fear</u> of <u>success</u>
4. Twenty-one days to make or break a habit
5. An easy natural course of actions: –your natural way of academic life
6. Synchronicity: – a reflection of a desired reality through your efforts
7. Fight for your academic grades in every way possible

AWAYS CONTINUE POLISHING YOUR DIAMOND – "The gleam in your bling"
1. Keep the confidence!
2. "I Intend to Play to Win!"
3. Maximize achievement!

4. Be strong!
5. Step high!
6. Work for "world class performance"!
7. Fight for superior academic grades achievement: – the unlimited values and unlimited opportunities! – Be strong!

As Dr. William Osler, the renowned physician and teacher, used to say to beginning medical students, "How can you take the greatest possible advantage of your capacities with the least possible strain?"(<u>as quoted in Armstrong, *Study is hard work,* p.23</u>) He answered the question in these words:

"By cultivating a system; I say cultivating advisedly, since some of you will find acquisition of systematic habits very hard. There are minds congeniality [born] systematic; others have a lifelong fight against an inherited tendency to diffuseness and carelessness in work. Take away with you, from a man who has had to fight a hard battle, the profound conviction of the value of system in your work. To follow the routine of the classes is easy enough, but to take routine into every part of your daily life is hard work. Let each hour of the day have its allotted duty, and cultivate that power of concentration which grows with its exercise, so that the attention neither flags nor wavers, but settles with bull-dog tenacity on the subject before you. Your constant repetition makes a good habit fit easily in your mind; and by the end of each class you may have gained that most precious of all knowledge – the power to work"

BE STRONG! is the positive reinforcement phrase to emphasize the management function of controlling. Controlling is setting performance standards, measuring actual performance, and taking corrective actions to achieve academic achievement goals (Bateman and Snell, *Management*, 2013, p.14).

CHAPTER 5

THE COLLEGE PERSPECTIVE

> *Daily Affirmation*
> "I am a good student. Any class I study, I can and will do very well. I intend to learn and perform at a high level of superior academic grades achievement. This is my opportunity in life. I will seize this moment".

According to (Gardner, Jewler, and Barefoot, 2004, p.9), "in the early 1900's fewer than two percent of Americans of traditional college age attended college. Today, new technologies and the information explosion are changing the workplace so drastically that to support themselves and their families adequately, most people will need some education beyond high school" (*Your College Experience, p.9*.

Also, stated by (Gardner, Jewler, and Barefoot, 2004) "Today approximately seventy percent of high school graduates go on to college, with more than 4000 colleges serving more than 14.8 million students. About one-third of those enrolling in college right after high school begin in two-year institutions. Adult students are also enrolling in record numbers, with more than thirty-seven percent of college students being over the age twenty-five. And college has become financially possible for nearly everyone, regardless of income. That's the bright side. The no-so-good side is that forty percent of students who start in four year programs never finish their degrees. In two-year colleges, half or more of the entering class will drop out by the end of the first year".

Of course, college will affect you in other ways. No matter what your major, you will emerge from college with a liberal education. (Facione,Peter,A., 2013, p.22) explains "Liberal education, as in to "liberate" or "free" signifies that a well-rounded college education will expand life's possibilities for you in the richness of how our world, our nation, our society, and its people came to be. Liberal education is about learning to learn and discovering how to think for yourself, both on your own and by collaborating with others. The result is that you will understand how to accumulate knowledge and will learn more about how to appreciate the cultural, artistic, and spiritual dimensions of life. You will be more likely to seek appropriate information before making a decision. Also, such information will help you realize how our lives are shaped by global as well as local political, social, psychological, economic, environmental, and physical forces. You will grow intellectually through interaction with cultures, languages, ethnic groups, religions, nationalities, and social classes other than your own" (Your College experience: *Strategies for Success*, p.6) and (Facione, Peter, A. Critical Thinking: *"What it is and why it counts"* [Milllbrae, CA:,Measured Reasons and The California Academic Press, p.22).

As confirmed by *Striving for Excellence in College: Tips for active Learning*:

> When we say excellent college student <u>we are</u> not presenting you with a model of college life that is beyond your grasp. Nor do <u>we</u> believe that college is nothing more that assignments and books, important though those are. Rather, <u>we</u> have in mind a student <u>who</u>, like you, is preparing for a life of continual learning and who knows that the primary habits of mind required for such a life require an understanding of how to squeeze out meaning from the confusing multitude of facts, ideas, and experiences. Central to this search for meaning is the ability to think critically, and to distinguish sense from relative nonsense. Almost any college student with the right attitude and training can be an excellent learner. Excellence in college is achieved gradually. Many individual attitudes and skills must be developed while attending class and studying. The goal is

reached <u>bit-by-bit;</u> so great patience is essential. (<u>Brown, M. Neil [New Jersey: Prentice Hall, 1997]p.3</u>)

As (Gardner, Jewler, and Barefoot write in *Your College Experience*: 2004 p.124)

"An essential goal of a college education is to cultivate a capacity for reflection about, and analysis of, issues of values of society and values in one's personal life. College is preparation for life as well as a career, and an opportunity for personal development, including-quite centrally-values development. It is vitally important to learn to integrate both intellectual development and personal values development. All too often, such an opportunity goes wasted".

Address any fears you may have:

> All that is necessary for such problems or thoughts is a practical response; something that acts certainly to remove or reduce adverse effect. Thinking of it that way, helps too. Try not to worry. No doom and gloom. It will be more likely to go well if you are sure it will do so – more so if you work at organizing matters so that every factor helps. (<u>Forsyth, Patrick, and</u>

Frances Kaye, *The Art of Successful Business* [UK: IET Publishers, 2010.] p.62).

Consider the poem "The Man Who Thinks He Can" by Walter D. Wintle:

>IF you think you are beaten, you are,
>If you think you dare not, you don't.
>If you like to win, but you think you can't,
>It's almost certain you won't
>If you think you'll lose, you've lost,
>For out in the world we find,
>Success begins with a fellows will;
>It's all in the state of mind.
>If you think you're outclassed, you are:
>You've got to think high to rise.
>You've got to be sure of yourself before
>You can ever win a prize.
>Life's battles don't always go
>To the stronger or faster man,
>But soon or late the man who wins,
>Is the man who thinks he can.

CHAPTER 6
CONCLUSION

Daily Affirmation

"I am a good student. Any class I study, I can and will do very well. I intend to learn and perform at a high level of superior academic grade achievement. This is my opportunity in life. I will seize this moment".

Maximize Achievement! is the reality illumination of the improvement that the management of academic achievement success has to create the brilliant opportunities for your future. The value of education is to realize that knowledge is powerful, and with imagination, your **opportunities are unlimited**. Realizing of your "Knowledge" power will enhance your desirable academic performance that reflects the gleaming beacon of opportunity in your academic and career life.

Academic performance is a wonderful phenomenon. Academic grade success is fun. When excellent *Maximize Achievement!* strategies are applied, they will create 'the gleam in your bling!; or the glow of your superior academic grades achievement. Excellent superior academic grades achievement is a winning, gleaming beacon that enhances a student to be recognized as a world-class performer. This is the brilliance of a competitive advantage illuminating and beaming for the world to see "the gleam in your bling!"

Notice that "the gleam in your bling" is not seen in your ear, nose, or finger. It is seen by all persons that witness the victory of your stellar academic performance.

As recommended by Armstrong and Lampe, accept the fact that learning is something that no one can do for you _(Study Tactics, 1983, p. 25)_. And remember:

> Learning is a lonely business, not a social affair. Even in the classroom, in the midst of your fellow students, you will be learning on your own. If you expect the class to be a social affair, you are bound to be disappointed. Learning anything of value is difficult, hard, often tedious work: but remember, it also has moments of joy and exhilaration arising from the feeling of achievement and self-satisfaction. (Armstrong, _Barron's Pocket Guide,_ p. 10)

CHAPTER 8
References

Armstrong, W. H., &Lampe II, M. W. (1983) Study Tactics – A Master Plan For Success In School, 2nd ed., Hauppauge, New York, NY, Barron's Educational Series, Inc.

Bateman, T. S., & Snell, S. A. (2013) Management – Leading & Collaborating in a Competitive World, 10th ed., New York, NY, McGraw-Hill Irwin, Inc.

Browne, M. N., & Keeley, S. (1997) Striving for Excellence in College, Upper Saddle River, NJ, Prentice-Hall, Inc.

Connelly, J., & Forsyth, P. (2010) The Study Skills Guide, Essential Strategies for Smart Students, Philadelphia, PA, USA, Kogan Page Limited

Daft, R. L. (2011) The Leadership Experience, 5th ed., Mason. Ohio, Thompson, South-Western, Inc.

Gardner, J. N., & Jewler, A. J. (2004) Your College Experience, Strategies for Success, Belmont, CA, Wadsworth/Thomson Learning

Hamacheck, A. L. (2002) Coping with College: A Guide for Academic Success, 2nd ed., Upper Saddle River, New Jersey, Pearson Education Inc.

Holschuh, J. P., & Nist-Olejnik, S. L. (2011) Effective College Learning, 2nd ed., Boston, MA, Pearson Education, Inc.

Koch, N. S., & Wasson, K. W. (2002) The Transfer Student's Guide to The College Experience, Boston, MA, Houghton Mifflin Co.

Mager, R. F. (1988) Making Instruction Work or Skillbloomers, Belmont, CA, Lake Publishing Co.

Mckowen, C. (1979) Get your "A" out of College-Mastering the hidden rules of the game, Los Altos, CA, Crisp Publications, Inc.

Pauk, W. (1993) How to Study in College, 5th ed., Boston, MA, Houghton Mifflin Co.

Pride, W. M., Hughes, R. J., & Kapoor, J. R. (2012) Business, 8th ed., Boston, MA, Houghton Mifflin Co.

Scharf, D., & Hait, P. ((1985) Studying Smart-Time Management for College Students, New York, NY, Harper & Row, Publishers

Zwier, L. J., & Mathes II, G. (2005) Study Skills for Success, Ann Arbor, MI, The University of Michigan

Dr. Paul B. Hudson, Biography

Dr. Paul B. Hudson is the son of Johnnie L. and Nannie Hudson, and a native of Benton Harbor, Michigan. After graduating from Benton Harbor High School, he enrolled at Western Michigan University in Kalamazoo, Michigan. There he achieved the degrees of a Bachelor of Business Administration and a Master of Human Resource Development. He has also achieved an additional Masters of Arts in Management degree at Nazareth College and another Masters of Business Administration degree at the University of Illinois at Springfield. His terminal academic achievement was a Doctor of Management degree at Webster University in St. Louis, Missouri.

Currently, he commands the position of full-time tenured faculty as "Professor of Business" at Lincoln Land Community College in Springfield, Illinois. He has held additional academic staff, professorship, and adjunct professorship positions at Western Michigan University, Kellogg Community College, Kalamazoo Valley Community College, Lake Michigan College, Davenport University, and University of Illinois at Springfield.

He has experience in entrepreneurship and executive management responsibilities in both the private and public sector. These executive management experiences span organizations such as City of Kalamazoo, Pitney Bowes Corporation, Colonial Engineering Company, Ameritech Corporation, National City Bank, private business ventures, and others.

Dr. Paul B. Hudson's academic life philosophy is that academic success is simply enhancing a student's vision of their academic achievement reality. A reality which will guide that student to successful college completion and graduation. For many years his presentations and lectures of – "I intend to Play to Win!", "Maximize Achievement!", "Step High!" & "Be Strong!" - are stimuli he directed toward students to create superior academic achievement and inspiration that will lead them to college graduation. That is the ultimate "call of academic service" to students.

Print and c Copyright by
Dr. Paul B. Hudson, D.Mgt.
All Rights Reserved (2016)
Maximize Achievement! CO.
Use the following,

Positive affirmations statements to support your mental images of your progress and academic success! Place this positive posture in your view for a daily reminder.

I
INTEND
TO
PLAY TO
WIN!

Positive affirmations statements to support your mental images of your progress and academic success! Place this positive posture in your view for a daily reminder.

Print and c Copyright by
Dr. Paul B. Hudson, D.Mgt.
ALL RIGHTS RESERVED (2016)
Maximize Achievement! CO.

Maximize Achievement!

Positive affirmations statements to support your mental images of your progress and academic success! Place this positive posture in your view for a daily reminder.

Print and c Copyright by
Dr. Paul B. Hudson, D.Mgt.
ALL RIGHTS RESERVED (2016)
Maximize Achievement! **CO.**

The gleam in your bling!

Positive affirmations statements to support your mental images of your progress and academic success! Place this positive posture in your view for a daily reminder.

Print and c Copyright by
Dr. Paul B. Hudson, D.Mgt.
ALL RIGHTS RESERVED (2015)
Maximize Achievement! **CO.**

STEP HIGH!

Positive affirmations statements to support your mental images of your progress and academic success! Place this positive posture in your view for a daily reminder.

Print and c Copyright by
Dr. Paul B. Hudson, D.Mgt.
ALL RIGHTS RESERVED (2016)
Maximize Achievement! **CO.**

BE STRONG!

Maximize Achievement!
(College Sense)

PLANNING

ORGANIZING

LEADING

CONTROLLING

ACADEMIC GOALS

Print and c Copyright by
Dr. Paul B. Hudson, D.Mgt.
ALL RIGHTS RESERVED (2013)
Maximize Achievement! CO.

Maximize Achievement! (College Sense) ACADEMIC READINESS GUIDE TO COLLEGE COMPLETION AND GRADUATION IS A MANAGEMENT OF A SELF-DIRECTED INNOVATIVE EDUCATIONAL ACHCHIEVEMENT STRATEGY. THIS GUIDE IS DESIGNED TO ASSIST ALL COLLEGE STUDENTS TO THAT END.

Maximize Achievement! CO.

Dr. Paul B. Hudson, is my name
Maximize Achievement! Is my claim to fame.
I'm not new to this game
I'm true to this game,
I'm in it to win it
And I intend to play to win.
And nine times out of ten
I'm going to do it again.
Get Back! Get Back! Get Back!
You got to do this
If you want to have stacks!
So, work real hard
To get good grades
To make "Your Future So Bright…"
"You GOTTA To Wear Shades"!
This is, Sealed for antiquity,
As you make your history;
That leads to your destiny.
And that's all I Got to Say!

Dr. Paul B. Hudson, BBA, MAM, MA, MBA, D.Mgt.

Work Real Hard to Get Good Grades
To
Make
Your Future So Bright…
You Gotta Wear Shades!
Dr. Paul B. Hudson, D.Mgt.

Order Form and Inquires: Website.com

CPSIA information can be obtained
at www.ICGtesting.com
Printed in the USA
FFHW020048091218
49817297-54339FF